W9-AVD-037

The AMAZING WORLD OF GUMBALL™

AFTER SCHOOL SPECIAL

ROSS RICHIE ....CEO & Founder
MATT GAGNON ....Editor-in-Chief
FILIP SABLIK ....President of Publishing & Marketing
STEPHEN CHRISTY ....President of Development
LANCE KREITER ....VP of Licensing & Merchandising
PHIL BARBARO ....VP of Finance
ARUNE SINGH ....VP of Marketing
BRYCE CARLSON .... Managing Editor
MEL CAYLO ....Marketing Manager
SCOTT NEWMAN ....Production Design Manager
KATE HENNING ....Operations Manager
SIERRA HAHN ....Senior Editor
DAFNA PLEBAN ....Editor, Talent Development
SHANNON WATTERS ....Editor
ERIC HARBURN ....Editor
WHITNEY LEOPARD ....Associate Editor
JASMINE AMIRI ....Associate Editor
CHRIS ROSA ....Associate Editor
ALEX GALER..Associate Editor
CAMERON CHITTOCK ....Associate Editor
MATTHEW LEVINE ....Assistant Editor
SOPHIE PHILIPS-ROBERTS ....Assistant Editor
KELSEY DIETERICH ....Production Designer
JILLIAN CRAB ....Production Designer
MICHELLE ANKLEY ....Production Designer
GRACE PARK ....Production Design Assistant
ELIZABETH LOUGHRIDGE ....Accounting Coordinator
STEPHANIE HOCUTT ....Social Media Coordinator
JOSÉ MEZA ....Sales Assistant
JAMES ARRIOLA ....Mailroom Assistant
HOLLY AITCHISON ....Operations Assistant
SAM KUSEK ....Direct Market Representative
AMBER PARKER ....Administrative Assistant

**THE AMAZING WORLD OF GUMBALL: AFTER SCHOOL SPECIAL
Scholastic Edition, January 2017.** Published by KaBOOM!, a division
of Boom Entertainment, Inc. THE AMAZING WORLD OF GUMBALL,
CARTOON NETWORK, the logos, and all related characters and
elements are trademarks of and © Turner Broadcasting System Europe
Limited, Cartoon Network. (S17) Originally published in single magazine
form as THE AMAZING WORLD OF GUMBALL 2015 Special No. 1, THE
AMAZING WORLD OF GUMBALL 2015 GRAB BAG SPECIAL No. 1, and THE
AMAZING WORLD OF GUMBALL 2016 GRAB BAG SPECIAL No. 1. © Turner
Broadcasting System Europe Limited, Cartoon Network. (S16) All rights
reserved. KaBOOM!™ and the KaBOOM! logo are trademarks of Boom
Entertainment, Inc., registered in various countries and categories.
All characters, events, and institutions depicted herein are fictional.
Any similarity between any of the names, characters, persons, events,
and/or institutions in this publication to actual names, characters,
and persons, whether living or dead, events, and/or institutions is
unintended and purely coincidental. KaBOOM! does not read or accept
unsolicited submissions of ideas, stories, or artwork.

For information regarding the CPSIA on this printed material, call:
(203) 595-3636 and provide reference #RICH – 718911. A catalog record
of this book is available from OCLC and from the BOOM! Studios
website, www.boom-studios.com, on the Librarians Page.

BOOM! Studios, 5670 Wilshire Boulevard, Suite 450, Los Angeles, CA
90036-5679. Printed in USA. First Printing.

ISBN: 978-1-68415-063-2, eISBN: 978-1-61398-740-7

THE AMAZING WORLD OF GUMBALL
AFTER SCHOOL SPECIAL

created by
Ben BOCQUELET

"THE HEADPHONES"
script by
ZACHARY CLEMENTE
art by
ANDY HIRSCH
colors by
FRED C. STRESING
letters by
SHAWN ALDRIDGE

"THE LAUNCH"
script & art by
ANDREW GREEN

"STORAGE UNIT"
script by
COHEN EDENFIELD
art by
KATE LETH

"ANAIS'S WAND"
script & art by
NNEKA MYERS

"STORIES FROM THE CEMETERY"
script & art by
PHILIP MURPHY

"GAME ON"
script & art by
TAIT HOWARD
colors & letters by
KATY FARINA

"CRAYON WAX ON, CRAYON WAX OFF"
script & art by
KATE SHERRON

"THE COLLECTION"
script by
FERNANDA JABER
art by
FELLIPE MARTINS

**"THE LEGENDARY LEADER
OF LAUNDRODOME"**
script & art by
ZACK GIALLONGO

"FUNLAND FIASCO"
script & art by
PHILIP MURPHY

"THE TREASURE ROOM"
script & art by
KATY FARINA

ads by
**YEHUDI MERCADO
PHILIP MURPHY**

pin ups by
**PHILIP MURPHY
MARIEL CARTWRIGHT
ZACK GIALLONGO
MISSY PENA
JENNA AYOUB**

designers
JILLIAN CRAB with **GRACE PARK**

assistant editors
**MARY GUMPORT
MATTHEW LEVINE**

editors
**SHANNON WATTERS
SIERRA HAHN**

"THE SHACK"
script & art by
ANNE SZABLA

"LUNCH TRADE"
script & art by
TERRY BLAS
letters by
WARREN MONTGOMERY

with special thanks to **MARISA MARIONAKIS,**
JANET NO, CURTIS LELASH, CONRAD
MONTGOMERY, MEGHAN BRADLEY
and the wonderful folks at **CARTOON NETWORK.**

THE HEADPHONES

The HEADPHONES

by Zachary Clemente
Illustrated by Andy Hirsch
Colors by Fred Stresing
Letters by Shawn Aldridge

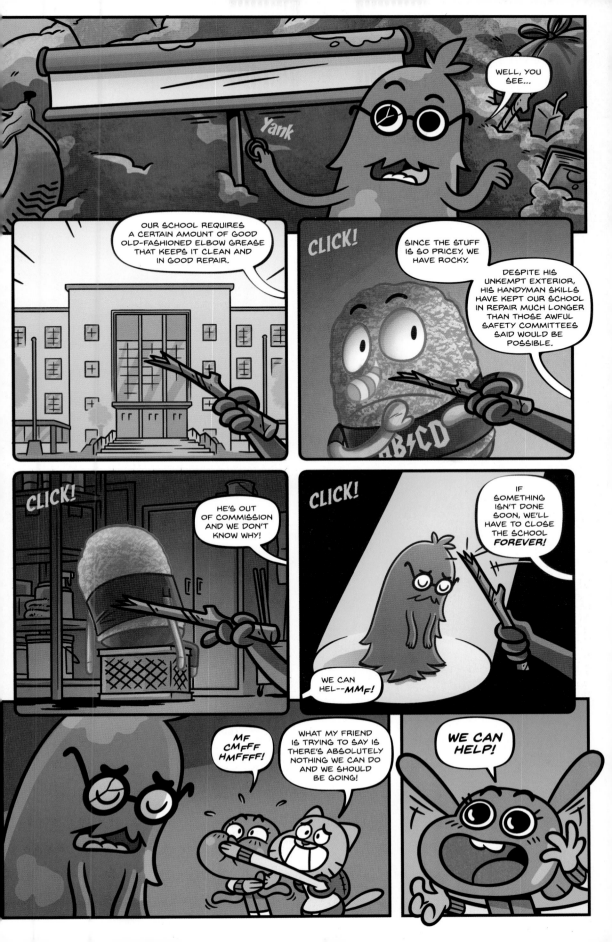

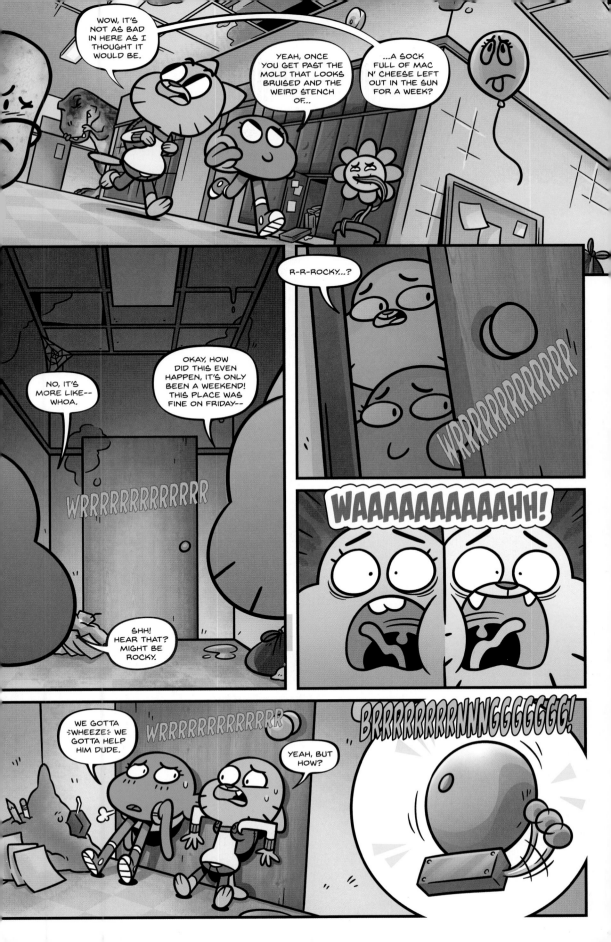

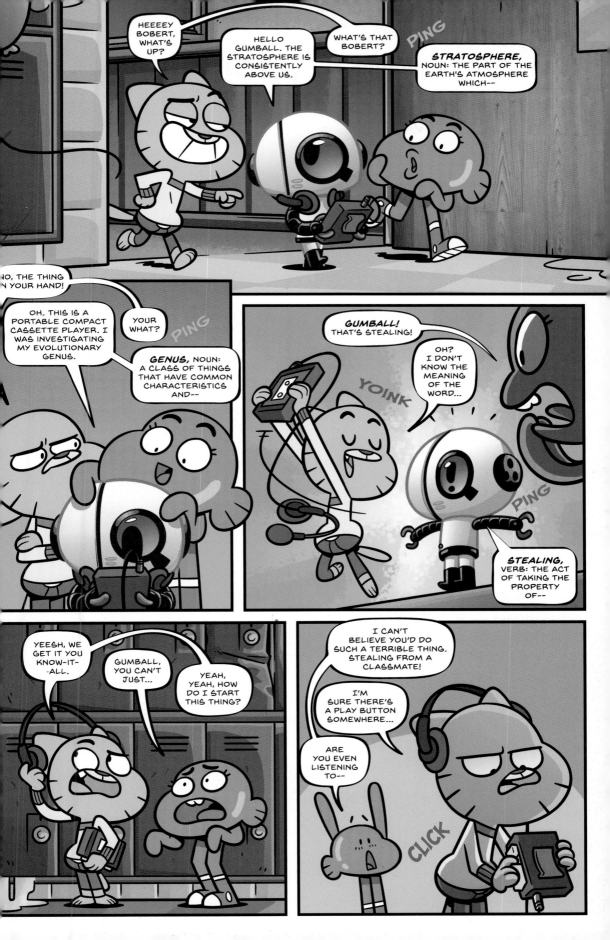

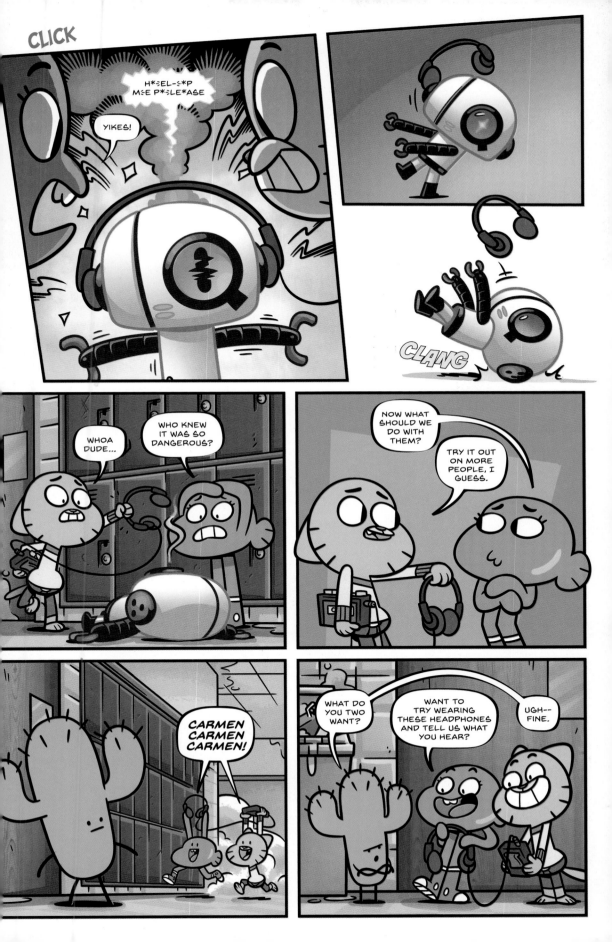

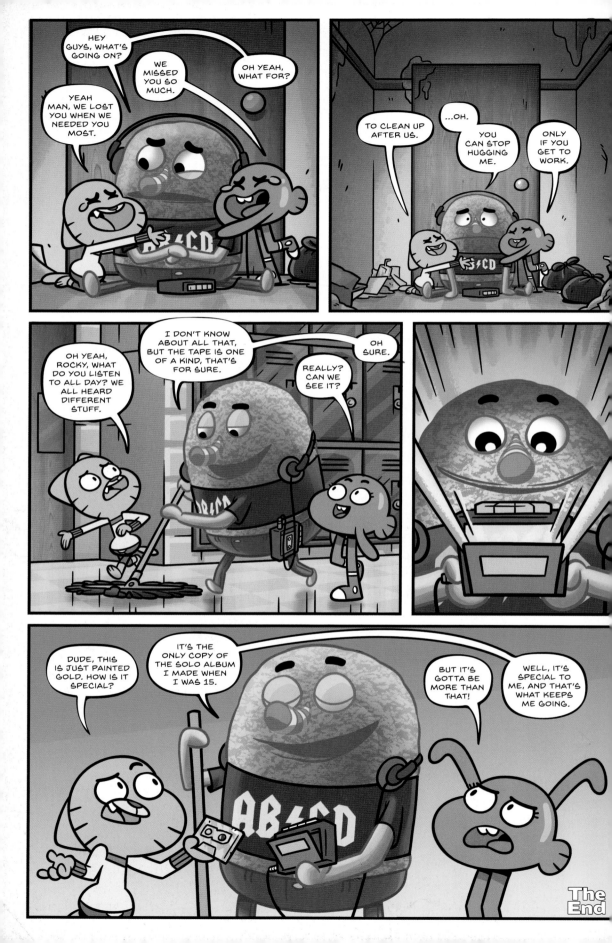

The End

THE LAUNCH

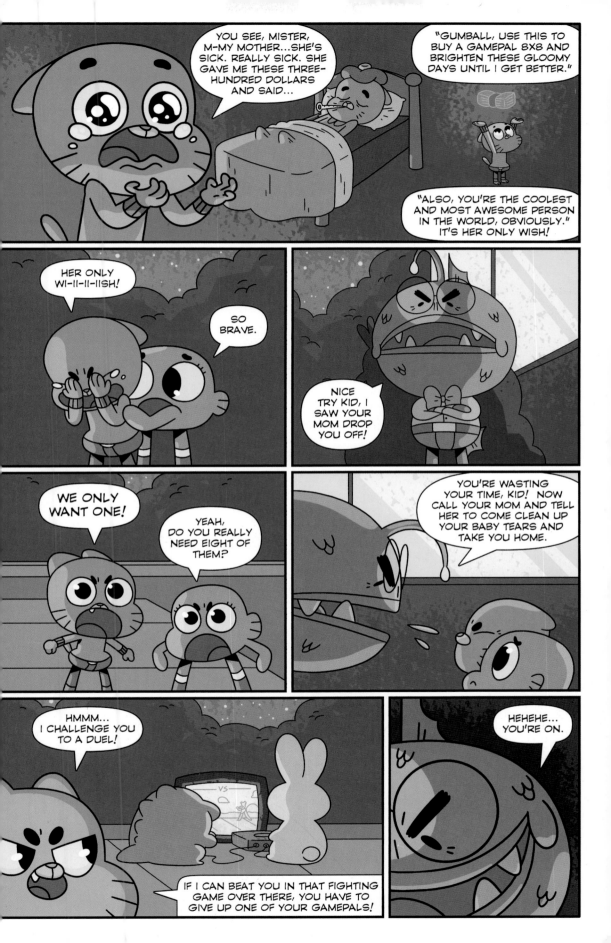

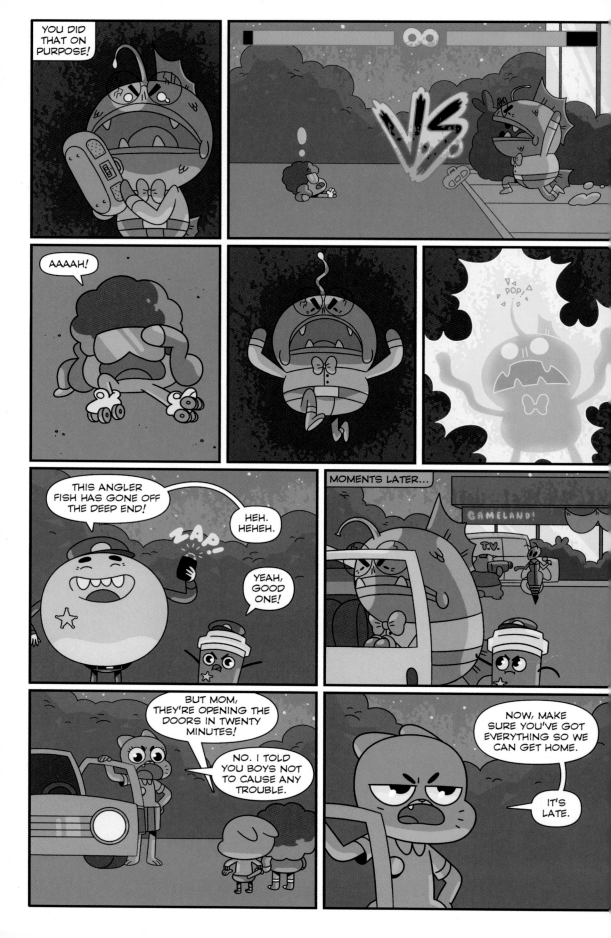

STORIES FROM
THE CEMETARY

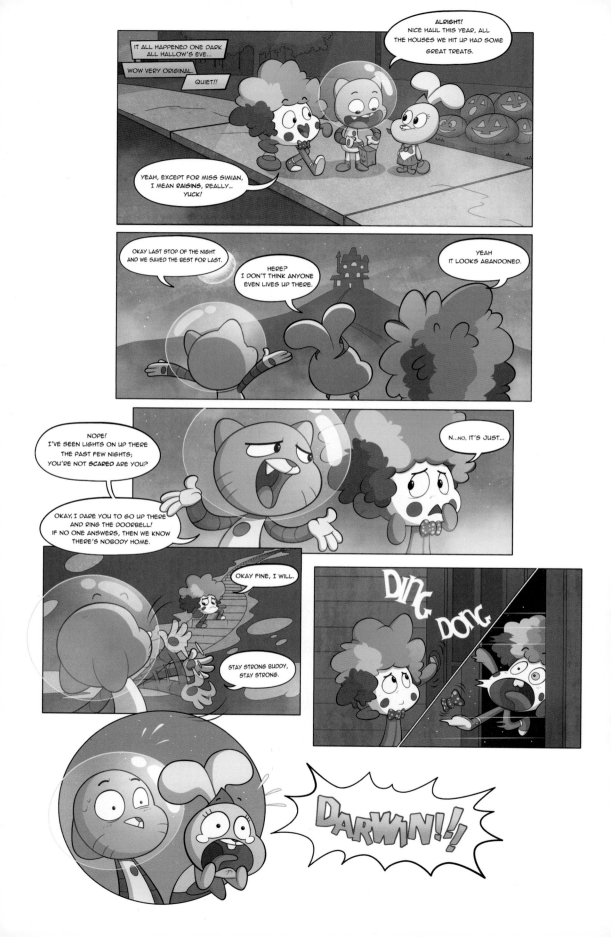

Pin-up by **PHILIP MURPHY**

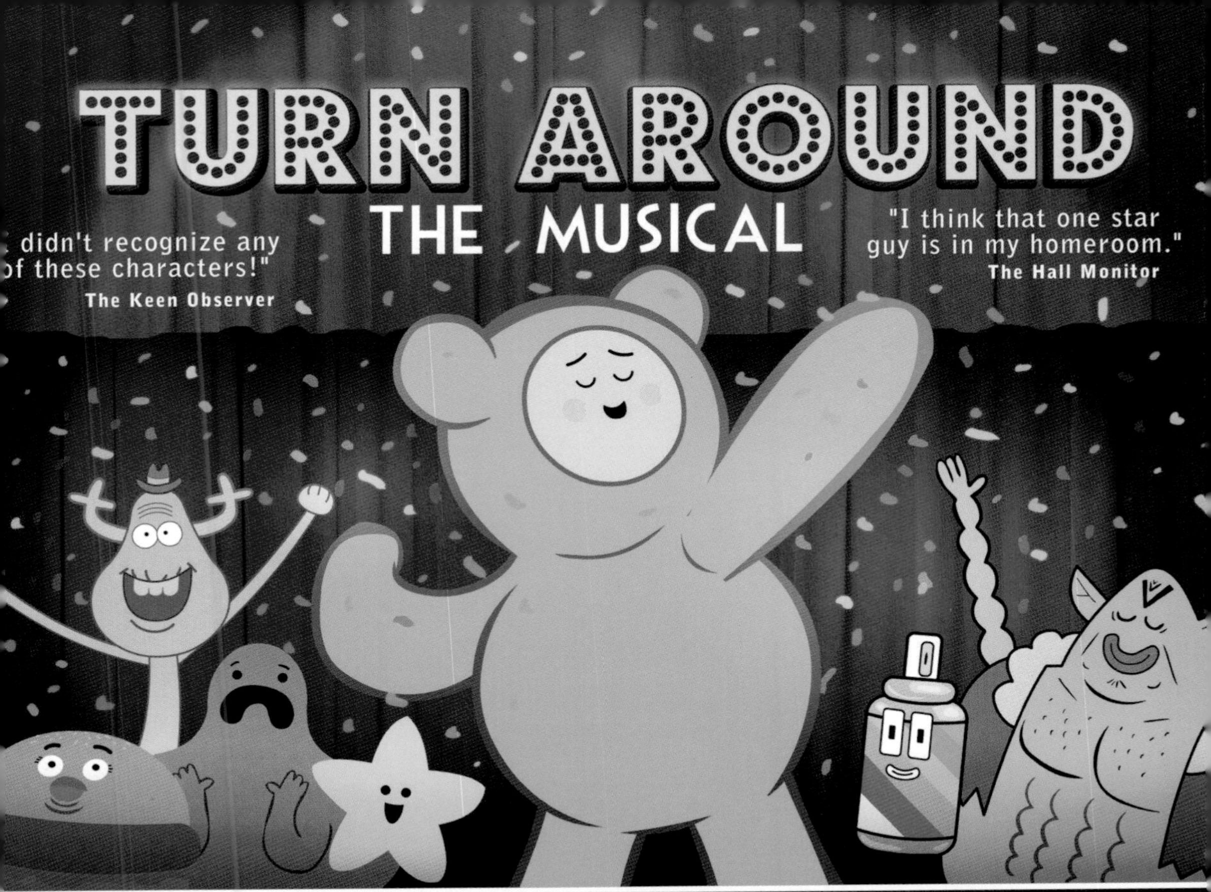

TURN AROUND
THE MUSICAL
didn't recognize any
of these characters!"
The Keen Observer
"I think that one star
guy is in my homeroom."
The Hall Monitor

DOPPLEGANGER 2
DOUBLE PUNCHER
Double the Quarters.
Double the Punching.
YEHUDI MERCADO

GAME ON

STORAGE UNIT

Pin-up by MARIEL CARTWRIGHT

ANAIS'S WAND

CRAYON WAX ON,
CRAYON WAX OFF

CRAYON WAX ON, CRAYON WAX OFF
by kate Sherron

THE COLLECTION

THE LEGENDARY LEADER
OF LAUNDRODOME

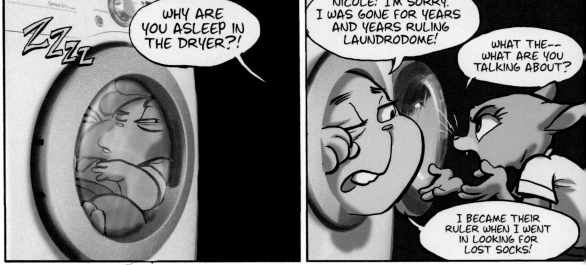

FUNLAND FIASCO

Pin-up by **MISSY PENA**

THE TREASURE ROOM

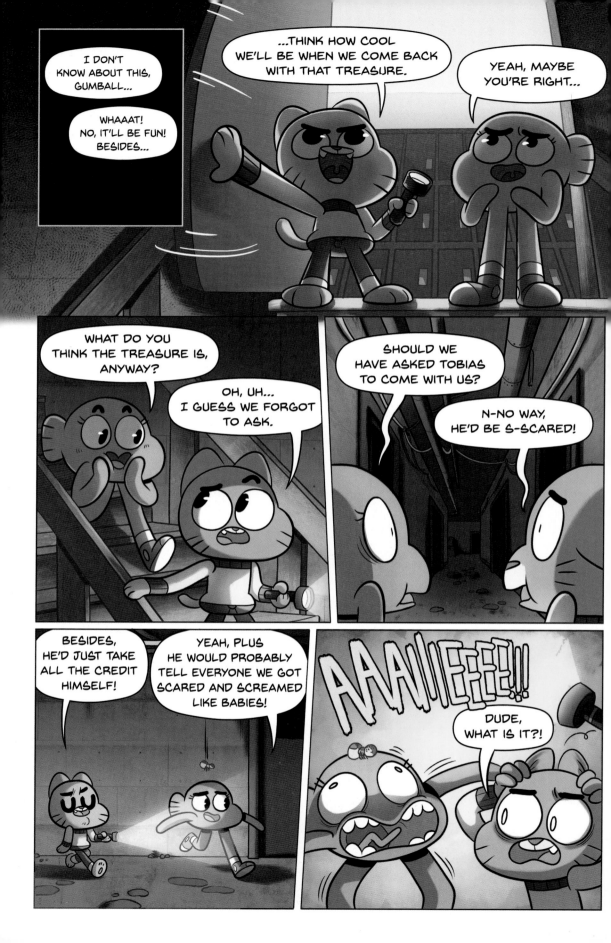

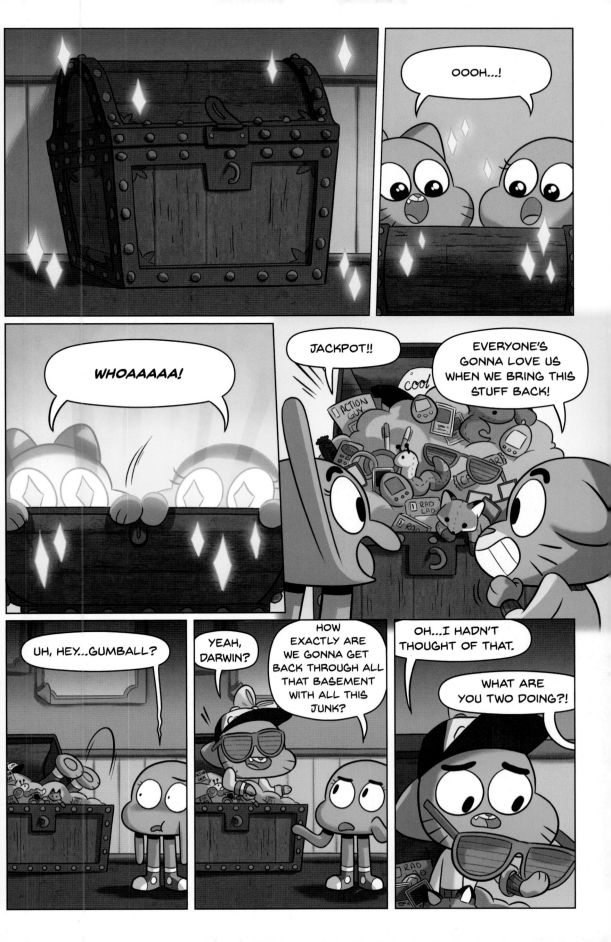

THE SHACK

Pin-up by **JENNA AYOUB**

LUNCH TRADE

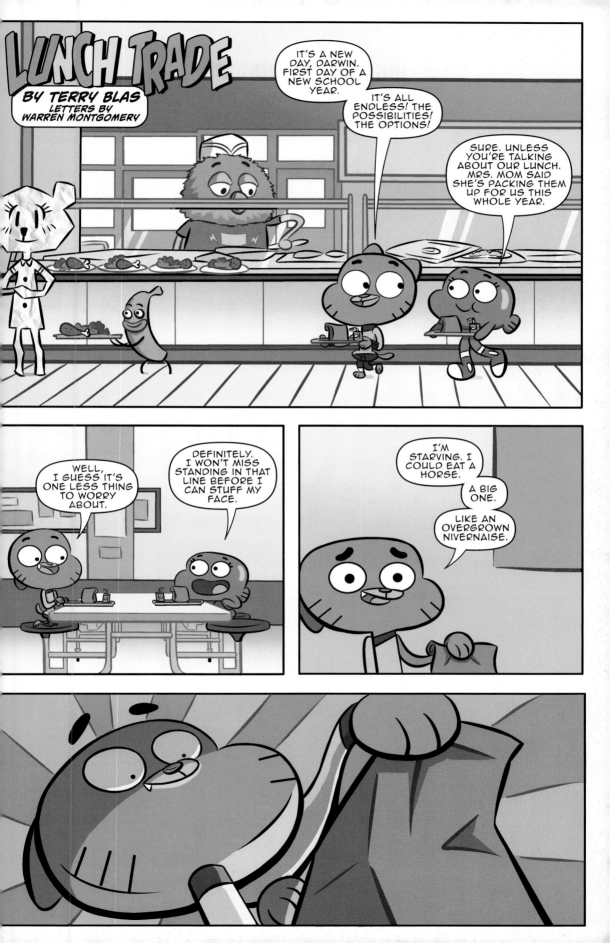

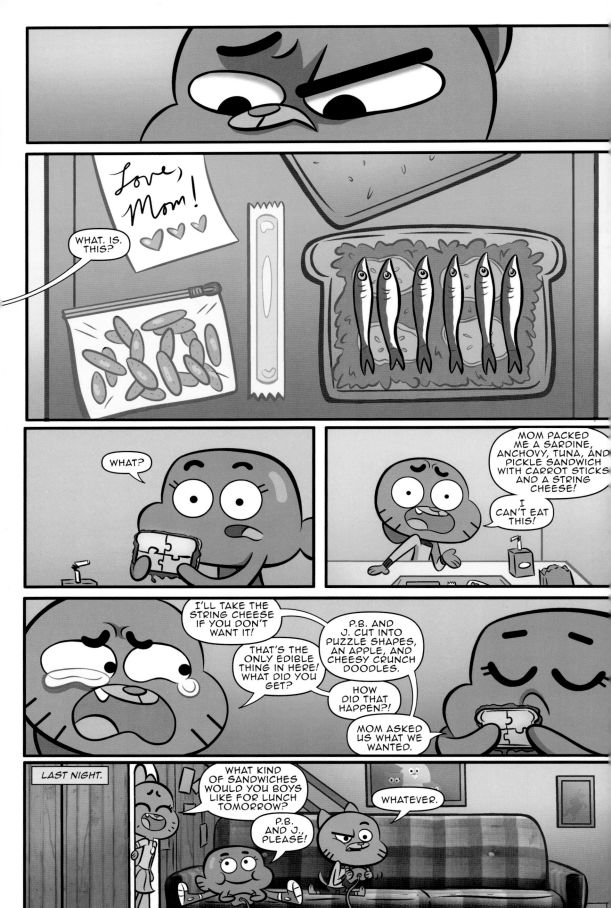

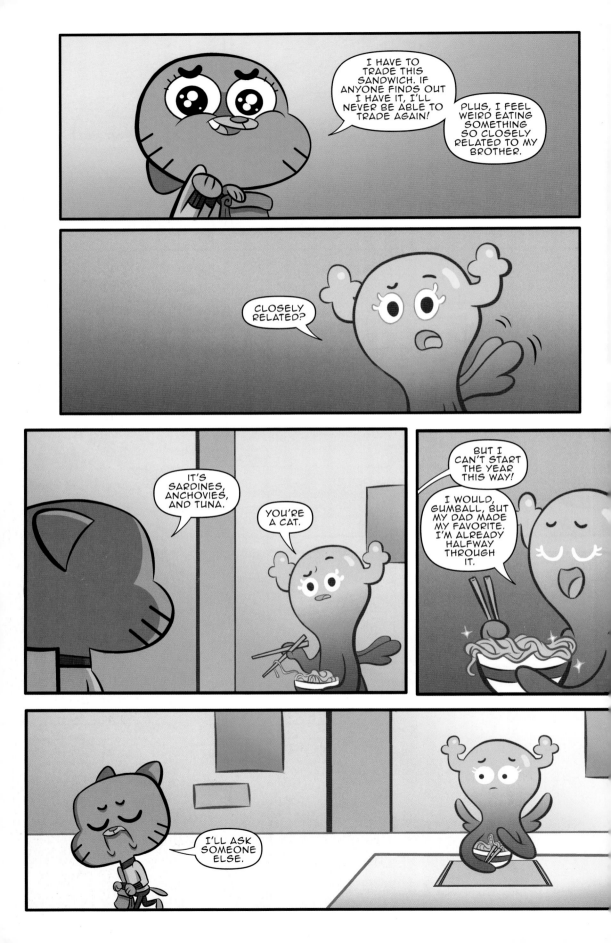